SELECTED FROM

GIANT
STEPS

KAREEM ABDUL-JABBAR
AND PETER KNOBLER

Supplementary material by the staff of
Literacy Volunteers of New York City

WRITERS' VOICES
Literacy Volunteers of New York City

WRITERS' VOICES℠ was made possible by grants from The Vincent Astor Foundation; Booth Ferris Foundation; Exxon Corporation; James Money Management, Inc.; Scripps Howard Foundation; Uris Brothers Foundation, Inc.; The H.W. Wilson Foundation; and Weil, Gotshal & Manges Foundation, Inc.

──────────**ATTENTION READERS**──────────

We would like to hear what you think about our books. Please send your comments or suggestions to:

The Editors
Literacy Volunteers of New York City
121 Avenue of the Americas
New York, NY 10013

Selection: From GIANT STEPS by Kareem Abdul-Jabbar and Peter Knobler. Copyright © 1983 by Kareem Abdul-Jabbar. Reprinted by permission of Bantam Books, a division of BANTAM, DOUBLEDAY, DELL PUBLISHING GROUP, INC.

Supplementary materials © 1990 by Literacy Volunteers of New York City Inc.

Printed in the United States of America.

96 95 94 93 92 91 90 10 9 8 7 6 5 4 3 2 1

First LVNYC Printing: April 1990

ISBN: 0-929631-10-2

Writers' Voices is a series of books published by Literacy Volunteers of New York City Inc., 121 Avenue of the Americas, New York, NY 10013. The words, "Writers' Voices," are a trademark of Literacy Volunteers of New York City.

Cover design by Paul Davis Studio; interior design by Barbara Huntley.
Publishing Director, LVNYC: Nancy McCord
Executive Director, LVNYC: Eli Zal

LVNYC is an affiliate of Literacy Volunteers of America.

ACKNOWLEDGMENTS

Literacy Volunteers of New York City gratefully acknowledges the generous support of the following foundations and corporations that made the publication of WRITERS' VOICES and NEW WRITERS' VOICES possible: The Vincent Astor Foundation; Booth Ferris Foundation; Exxon Corporation; James Money Management, Inc.; Scripps Howard Foundation; Uris Brothers Foundation, Inc.; The H.W. Wilson Foundation; and Weil, Gotshal & Manges Foundation Inc.

This book could not have been realized without the kind and generous cooperation of the author, Kareem Abdul-Jabbar, and his publisher, Bantam Books Inc.

We deeply appreciate the contributions of the following suppliers: Cam Steel Rule Die Works Inc. (steel cutting die for display); Canadian Pacific Forest Products Ltd. (text stock); Creative Graphics, Inc. (text typesetting); Horizon Paper Co., Inc. (cover stock); Martin/Friess Communications (display header); Mergenthaler Container (corrugated display); Phototype Color Graphics (cover color separations); and Ringier America Dresden Division (cover and text printing and binding).

For their guidance and assistance, we wish to thank the LVNYC Board of Directors' Publishing Committee: James E. Galton, Marvel Entertainment Group; Virginia Barber, Virginia Barber Literary Agency, Inc.; Jeff Brown; George P. Davidson, Ballantine Books; Geraldine E. Rhoads, Diamandis Communications Inc.; Virginia Rice, Reader's Digest; Martin Singerman, News America Publishing, Inc.; and Irene Yuss, Pocket Books.

Thanks also to Caron Harris and Steve Palmer of

Ballantine Books for production assistance, Jeff Brown for his editorial skill and advice, Barbara A. Mancuso of The New York Times Pictures for her help in researching our cover illustration, and Sergei Boissier for proofreading.

Our thanks to Paul Davis Studio and Myrna Davis, Paul Davis, and Jeanine Esposito for their inspired design of the covers of WRITERS' VOICES. Thanks also to Barbara Huntley for her sensitive attention to the interior design of this series.

And finally, special credit must be given to Marilyn Boutwell, Jean Fargo, and Gary Murphy of the LVNYC staff for their major contributions to the educational and editorial content of these books.

CONTENTS

ABOUT *WRITERS' VOICES*

"I want to read what others do—what I see people reading in libraries, on the subway, and at home."

Mamie Moore, a literacy student,
Brooklyn, New York

Writers' Voices is our response to Mamie Moore's wish:

- the wish to step forward into the reading community,
- the wish to have access to new information,
- the wish to read to her grandchildren,
- the wish to read for the joy of reading.

NOTE TO THE READER

"What we are familiar with, we cease to see. The writer shakes up the familiar scene, and, as if by magic, we see a new meaning in it." Anaïs Nin

Writers' Voices invites you to discover new meaning. One way to discover new meaning is to learn something new. Another is to see in a new way something you already know.

Writers' Voices is a series of books. Each book contains selections from one or more writer's work. We chose the selections because the writers' voices can be clearly heard. Also, they deal with experiences that are interesting to think about and discuss.

If you are a new reader, you may want to have a selection read aloud to you, perhaps more than once. This will free you to enjoy the piece, to hear the language used, and to think about its meaning.

Even if you are a more experienced reader, you may enjoy hearing the selection read aloud before reading it silently to yourself.

Each selection is set in a framework to expand your understanding of the selection. The framework includes a chapter that tells about the writer's life. Some authors write about their own lives; others write stories from their imagination. You may wonder why an author chose to write what he or she did. Sometimes you can find the answer by knowing about the author's life.

You may also find chapters about the characters, the plot, and when or where the story took place. These will help you begin thinking about the selection. They will also help you understand what may be unfamiliar to you.

We encourage you to read *actively*. An active reader does many things—while reading, and before and after reading—that help him or her better understand and enjoy a book. Here are some suggestions of things you can do:

Before Reading

• Read the front and back covers of the book, and look at the cover illustration. Ask yourself what you expect the book to be about, based on this information.

• Think about why you want to read this book. What do you want to discover, and what questions do you hope will be answered?

• Look at the contents page. Decide which chapters you want to read and in what order you want to read them.

During Reading

• Try to stay with the rhythm of the language. If you find any words or sentences you don't understand, keep reading to see if the meaning becomes clear. If it doesn't, go back and reread the difficult part or discuss it with others.

• Try to put yourself into the story.

• Ask yourself questions as you read. For example: Do I believe this story or this character? Why?

After Reading

• Ask yourself if the story makes you see any of your own experiences in a new way.

• Ask yourself if the story has given you any new information.

• Keep a journal in which you can write down your thoughts about what you have read, and save new words you have learned.

• Look over the questions at the end of the book. They are meant to help you discover more about what you have read and how it relates to you—as a person, as a reader, and as a writer. Try those questions that seem most interesting to you.

• Talk about what you have read with other readers.

Good writing should make you think after you put the book down. Whether you are a beginning reader, a more experienced reader, or a teacher of reading, we encourage you to take time to think about these books and to discuss your thoughts with others. If you want to read more books by the author of the selections, you can go to your bookstore or library to find them.

When you are finished with the book, we hope you will write to our editors about your reactions. We want to know your thoughts about our books, and what they have meant to you.

ABOUT THE SELECTIONS FROM *GIANT STEPS*

In preparing the story of his life, *Giant Steps*, Kareem Abdul-Jabbar worked with a professional writer named Peter Knobler. Knobler says in the foreword to the book, "We spent a lot of time together, four or five hours a day for a month or more, talking into a tape recorder about the course of his life."

Kareem didn't tell his life story exactly as it appears here. Probably he told about people and events as they came to mind. When the stories on the tapes were typed up, Knobler put them into an order that gave an accurate account of Kareem's life and opinions.

In this autobiography, Kareem talks about the people who have been important to him: his parents; the great Wilt Chamberlain; his coach at UCLA, John Wooden; the players he played with and against.

Places have also been very important to Kareem. He explains the education about life that he received on the streets of New York City. He tells how much he liked the sunny warm climate of southern California. And he tells how isolated he felt in the cold midwestern city of Milwaukee.

When you read or listen to these selections from *Giant Steps*, you will learn many of Kareem's opinions: about the need for stipends for college athletes, about the physical and mental pressures of professional sports, about religion, about the racism of a system in which most players are black and most owners and coaches are white.

In the last section, Kareem tells about a transformation, a change that happened to him. Working on his book had helped him to become more open and comfortable talking with people.

In these selections, Kareem Abdul-Jabbar tells about events in his personal and professional life over many years, from childhood through 1984. Perhaps you will have certain opinions in common with him. Perhaps you will want now to recall what you already know about Kareem Abdul-Jabbar, and then read to see if his experiences and opinions are what you expected.

If you would like to read more information about Kareem, please see the chapter "About Kareem Abdul-Jabbar," on page 54.

A TIMELINE FOR
KAREEM ABDUL-JABBAR

1947 Lew Alcindor born in New York City
1961 entered Power Memorial Academy
1965 entered UCLA
1968 converted to Islam
1969 signed with Milwaukee Bucks
1971 changed name to Kareem Abdul-Jabbar
       (from Lew Alcindor)
1975 signed with Los Angeles Lakers
1989 retired from pro basketball

HIGHLIGHTS OF
KAREEM'S PRO CAREER

NBA Most Valuable Player: 1971, 1972, 1974, 1976, 1977, 1980

League Leader in Scoring: 1971, 1972

League Leader in Blocked Shots: 1975, 1976, 1979, 1980

League Leader in Rebounds: 1976

League Leader in Field-Goal Percentage: 1977

Member of NBA Championship Team: 1971, 1980, 1982, 1985, 1987, 1988

MAP OF PLACES MENTIONED IN THE SELECTIONS

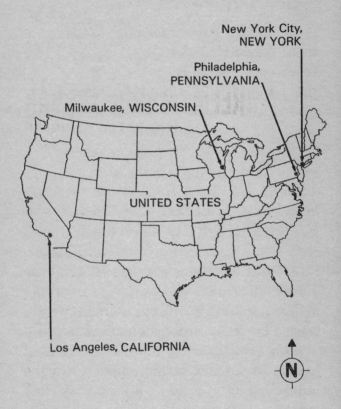

New York City, NEW YORK

Philadelphia, PENNSYLVANIA

Milwaukee, WISCONSIN

UNITED STATES

Los Angeles, CALIFORNIA

N

SELECTED FROM

GIANT STEPS

KAREEM ABDUL-JABBAR
AND PETER KNOBLER

When I was born in 1947, my parents were living in Harlem. Housing was scarce in New York after World War II, and when my father, Ferdinand Lewis "Al" Alcindor, got out of the Army he joined my mother, Cora, in something called "rooming." One person would rent a large apartment wherever it could be found and then let out individual rooms to friends, acquaintances, anyone who had the money. My mother had talked her way into getting not one but two front rooms in an eight-room apartment they shared with six other tenants on West 111th Street, just a block north of Central Park. When I was born I had my own room, and it's been that way basically ever since.

Harlem back then was by no means Paradise, but it wasn't the war zone it is today. When I was growing up, everyone around us had a job; to be on welfare was an embarrassment. My mother would take me to play in Central Park with no fear. People would leave their front doors open. Stealing was not tolerated. Anybody who got caught snatching a purse got handled by the people in the community. Some of the worst offenders would get thrown off the roof. People didn't play around.

My parents and I moved to the Dyckman Street projects in the Inwood section of Manhattan in 1950. It was city-owned middle-income housing and, although the City Housing Authority offered us another apartment on the Lower East Side, my mother waited a year and a half while the projects were being built so we could be in there first. It was a better neighborhood, she insisted.

* * *

School was very important in my home. My father was interested in my report cards, and my mother was vitally concerned. She wanted the best of everything—for her, for me, for our family—and saw schooling as the key to my future. There was no desperation; it wasn't like I had to lead my family out of the darkness— we were neither poor nor ignorant. What my mother carried in herself and instilled in me was ambition. With my father's respect for order, and my mother's vision of success, I was primed to do well in Catholic school [St. Jude's], and I did. I learned to read early and quickly. My homework got done because my mother made me do it, and after she'd drilled it into me how important it was, I did it for myself.

I never felt like I was black until I was made to. For fourth grade, whether to save money or work out some personal problems or just to live their lives without a nine-year-old boy underfoot—I've never been sure why—my parents sent me to an all-black boarding school in [Philadelphia] Pennsylvania, and I learned about being black in a hurry. Up until that point, color had not been a major issue. It wasn't ignored, we weren't living in any dream world, but race had not been the sole determining factor in what my life had been like. I'd been more apt to play with someone who was friendly than with someone who was black.

Nineteen fifty-six was a hard year for me. At five feet eight inches, I was bigger than all but one boy in the school, but at nine years old, I was as tough as almost none of them. It was as my first time away from home, my first experience in an all-black situation, and I found myself being punished for doing everything I'd ever been taught was right. I got all A's and was hated for it; I spoke correctly and was called a punk. I had to learn a new language simply to be able to deal with the threats. I had good manners and was a good little boy and paid for it with my hide.

About the only place I was even semi-safe was on the basketball court. In New York my father had shown me how to get the ball up to the basket ("This is how you protect the ball," he'd say, and elbow me in the face), and I had fooled around in the playground by myself, but at Holy Providence basketball was the only thing you could do, and since I was the second tallest guy in the school, I was automatically on the team. One of the local Catholic men would pile us in his car and take us to a seminary nearby where we would play against other Catholic elementary schools. It was organized ball but just barely, crazy games with kids running wild up and down the court. I was playing with boys older but smaller than myself, and where they were comfortable with their bodies, I didn't know what to do with mine.

But one day I stumbled upon a strange and delightful experience, kind of like that exciting yet amazingly unexpected feeling you get when you know, quite definitely, that you've entered puberty. In the first half, I was in the game, which was already unusual, and a rebound fell my way near the right of the basket. I fumbled with it, trying to conquer the dribble, and it almost got away. Finally, with a guy from the other team at my back, I looked over my shoulder, saw the basket, turned into the lane, and with one hand put up my first hook shot. It missed. Hit the back rim and bounced out. But it felt right, and the next time I got the ball I tried it again. Neither of them went in, but I had found my shot. At halftime my teammates, surprised that I had showed some coordination, encouraged me to practice it, and from then on, whenever I got into play I would shoot it. Nobody showed me how, it came naturally.

Lew came back to New York City and went through eighth grade at St. Jude's. Because of his size, many high schools recruited him. He chose Power Memorial Academy in New York City, which was well known for its basketball teams.

Nowadays white people know about the Rucker Tournament. It has been discovered and duly noted by the press as a summerlong meeting ground between professional basketball players and the uptown playground types. But back then you either had to be a ballplayer or have a serious tan to be hip to it. Holcombe L. Rucker, a black social worker, had created the tourney in 1946 as a means of getting attention for the Harlem brand of ball and getting the attention of the guys who played it. Just as white college basketball was patterned and regimented like the lives awaiting its players, the black schoolyard game demanded all the flash, guile, and individual reckless brilliance each man would need in the world facing him. This was on-the-job training when no jobs were available. No wonder these games were so intense, so consuming and passionate. For a lot of the men on that court this was as good as it was ever going to get, and it was winner-stay-on.

I met Wilt Chamberlain at the Rucker Tournament.

The first time was when I was fifteen, a freshman in high school six feet ten inches tall. I'd gone up to the St. Nicholas project on 129th Street between Seventh and Eighth Avenues where the Rucker Tournament was held, to watch. I was too timid, skinny, and nowhere near good enough to get in a game, but I needed to know how this thing was really played. I was up there with my friend Wesley Carpenter who lived all the way uptown, and we spotted Wilt, all of twenty-five years old and a Rucker celebrity, at midcourt taking off his street clothes to reveal his tank-top and uniform shorts underneath. There were only two men for me to be like in the NBA, Wilt and [Bill] Russell (clearly I couldn't be Oscar Robertson, Elgin Baylor, or Jerry West), and here was one of them, not so very much larger than I was, standing on the same blacktop. I didn't move, couldn't find anything to say that wasn't dumb. But Wesley was an outgoing guy, had a lot of nerve. He said, "Come on, let's just go meet him." I would never have done it alone.

Wes decided he would make the introductions since it was obviously beyond me. I told Wilt my name, and he said, "Oh yeah, I heard of you. You're that young boy that plays for the Catholic school, supposed to be getting good." Wilt had heard about me! When I thought about it later I got all charged up, but right then I was cool.

"I really admire the way you play the game," I told him, shaking his hand. He looked me up and down like a trainer examining a racehorse. "You've got good legs," he said. I looked down, trying to see what Wilt saw in me. He folded his shirt and pants, then turned back to me. "I wish I had legs like that," he said. I was thrilled—Wilt had taken notice of me!—and when the conversation died I just said, "Nice to meet you," and turned off into the crowd. From then on when I saw him at the Rucker I'd go up and have a few words.

I got close to Wilt that summer [1964]. He lifted weights at the 135th Street Y and I made a point of dropping in whenever I heard he was around. Once when I was shooting the ball in the gym, Wilt came by and we started playing some HORSE, matching shots, him trying to hit some hooks and me taking the fadeaways. We didn't go one-on-one, I wasn't even tempted, but at least now I had a speaking relationship with him.

You could tell when Wilt was at Small's [Small's Paradise was a jazz club that Chamberlain owned] because his black limo or his fuchsia Bentley would be sitting like a high-gloss sentinel out on the street, and it gave us a nice boost the first month just knowing he was in the territory. Small's was heaven for me, a black focal point for two of my favorite pursuits: jazz and basketball. And the pinpoint focus was Wilt.

Wilt was the only star I knew, and I stood in awe of him. He lived the life of public success, and I'd hang around Small's and watch how that worked. I had the good reputation—All-American, national champion—and it turned out that Wilt and the guys had been following my career, partly because I was a New Yorker and perhaps because sooner or later I would run up against Wilt, and his underlings were secretly tickled to think some young kid might give their boss a hard time. But when they met me and found out I wasn't one of those cocky loudmouths but a silent observer type, they took a liking to me, and I found myself a Small's regular.

With Lew starting, Power was voted the number one Catholic high school team for two years in a row. Lew was a high school All-American. Now he had to decide on a college and the course of his future.

I could go anywhere. Large school, small school, Ivy League, Big Ten, established basketball program or up-and-coming, they had all written the requisite letters, sent the materials, stood ready to make their pitch.

I wanted to play good, winning basketball at an institution that treated its athletes with an element of dignity, under a coach whom I could respect. I wasn't looking to turn anyone's program around, to save anything or anybody. I didn't want to be the first black athlete at a school, or the last. And I wanted someplace that was fun. I was looking to get out of the house and stay out.

My final four were distilled to the University of Michigan, Columbia, St. John's, and UCLA.

I went and visited the University of California at Los Angeles, and that settled that.

UCLA was gorgeous. They showed me a twenty-minute walk I'd have across campus to my classes, and I saw that, if I wanted, I could stroll the whole way on fresh green grass. It was sunny and warm and open, and I couldn't imagine why anyone would willingly live anywhere else.

The basketball inducements were not to be ignored, either. UCLA had just won the national championship for the second time in a row. The players themselves had become campus heroes. Pauley Pavilion, a mammoth new athletic arena that could hold 13,000 screaming Bruin fans, had already been erected and was standing there waiting for its convocation.

But most of all, what UCLA offered was John Wooden. Coach Wooden's office was about the size of a walk-in closet. I was brought in, and there was this very quaint-looking midwesterner, gray hair with a part almost in the middle of his head, glasses on. I'd heard a lot about this man and his basketball wisdom, but he surely did look like he belonged in a one-room schoolhouse. He stood up, shook my hand, and invited me to sit down.

He was quiet, which was a relief because so was I. I am a great believer in my own snap judgments, and I am quick to find major fault in minor offenses, particularly in strangers who need me, but I found myself liking Mr. Wooden right away. He was calm, in no hurry to impress me with his knowledge or his power. He could have made me cool my heels, or jumped up and been my buddy, but he clearly worked on his own terms, and I appreciated that in the first few moments we met. His suit jacket was hanging from a peg on the wall, and he was working in shirt-sleeves, casual but not far from decorum. He called me Lewis, and that decision endeared him to me even more; it was at once formal, my full name—We are gentlemen here—and respectful. I was no baby Lewie. Lewis. I liked that.

"We expect our boys to work hard and do well with their schoolwork," he told me in his flat yet not uninviting midwestern twang, "and I know you do have good grades so that should not be a problem for you. We expect you to be at practice on time and work hard while you're there. We do not expect our boys to present any disciplinary problems, but, again, we know you're not that kind of young man, and I don't expect you will have any difficulty here at UCLA.

"You've seen the campus. Do you have any questions?"

"I like the campus very much," I told him, "and I am very impressed with UCLA's basketball program."

"That's all very good," Coach Wooden said, "but I am impressed by your grades. You could do very well here as a student, whether you were an athlete or not. That is important. We work very hard to have our boys get through and earn their degrees. I hope all my student-athletes can achieve that. It is to both our benefits; your being a good student will keep you eligible to play in our basketball program, and your degree will be of value to you for the rest of your life."

People would always tell me that they cared about me, but I felt Mr. Wooden really meant it. I came out of his office knowing I was going to UCLA.

* * *

Coaches fan out over the personality spectrum. Some are disciplinarians who demand respect through fear, others try to be pals and gain it through affection. In all cases a coach's bottom line is respect because once a player is on the court, he must run his coach's plays, roll out his coach's system, with an overwhelming confidence. If the players do not respect the man and the intelligence that calls the shots, they will not perform at their peak. A player must perform for his coach; a coach must inspire performance in his players.

Coach Wooden made us unbeatable in one of the last games of our initial homestand. We were playing Colorado State and having a very hard time. They were big, they ran well, they had good scorers at every position. Late in the game we were only up by a basket. But Coach Wooden just took over. He had created the system that had made us a success so far, but this was the first time we needed him for some on-the-spot creativity, and as we listened he came through. He was always a precise speaker, but in the huddle he enunciated just a little more clearly, spoke a little more loudly. His eyes seemed even more sharply focused; he was *all there*. He called a play and we ran out there, and it worked! He called our defense, and they turned the ball over. He took control of the game. We put ourselves in his hands, and he taught us then and there how to win. He guided us when we really needed it, demonstrated his confidence, then instilled it in us; we'd do it his way, and we would win.

He used his mind, and he understood the game totally. The best he could do was the best there was. We won that game through a combination of technique and will, and for the next three years our confidence in him never wavered. He hadn't earned our respect, he'd defined it.

* * *

I felt then, and I feel now, that college athletes should be given at least a stipend in return for the services they render to a university. Walk-on athletes, those who pay their own tuition and try out for teams simply for the pleasure of playing, are one thing; they make their own choices. But scholarship athletes, who are recruited by the schools for the express purpose of playing ball, should be paid. A university with a winning team in a major sport like basketball or football is going to make tremendous amounts of money from admissions, concession sales, and television revenues. Alumni contributions rise substantially when the teams are winning, as a result of exposure and prestige. The athletes are in large part responsible for these huge influxes of cash yet not only are they prohibited from sharing in the fruits of their labor, as it stands now, they are often asked to put in both a full day in the classroom and a full day on the field. It's a tough load to carry, and being chronically short of cash doesn't help. That's why you hear of so many bogus jobs and under-the-table arrangements between players and boosters.

At the very least, scholarship athletes should be given a stipend that is sufficient for them to live comfortably, including room, board, and transportation. If you gave them what they deserve, you'd have to give them salaries; they put in a lot of hours and are highly skilled people in a high-visibility arena. Those few who go on to play professional sports have used college as a training ground for well-paying, if not necessarily extended, careers. Those who are not so fortunate—that large percentage of starting offensive linemen or defensive backs, or guards, centers, and forwards—have had their talents used by the schools to great monetary advantage, with nothing monetary to show for their efforts. A college education is rarely foremost in any of the principals' minds when a school's recruiter offers a high school athlete a scholarship. It's emotion on one side and dollars on the other. The dollars should be divided more evenly.

* * *

Malcolm X, who was a profound influence on me, had himself been guided by his faith in Islam.

I read Malcolm and then read the Qur'an.

At first I was fascinated, then fully absorbed. Islam was a religion a large portion of whose believers were black and which touched on all of my concerns. I saw myself as a victim of racism, and here first Malcolm and then the religion itself are pointing out immediately that racism is wrong. It says in the Qur'an: "We created you from one parent, and we created differences so that you may know one another." The parent was Adam, the differences were ethnic and cultural variety and the one source, Allah. Not only was this preached, it was practiced widely, throughout the world. When I found this out, I said to myself, "Hey, this is the way people are supposed to live. This is it!" From that point on I was sold.

In New York that summer of 1968 I started to learn Islam in earnest. I had found through my studies that the two largest Islamic groups were the Sunnites (450 million) and the Shi'ites (30 million). The Sunnites live mostly in Arabia, Afghanistan, Pakistan, Turkey, North Africa, Indonesia, and India; and the Shi'ites live mostly in Iran and Iraq. Largely because Malcolm X had been a Sunnite Muslim when he died, I chose the Sunnites.

When Lew played varsity basketball at UCLA, the school won three straight NCAA championships. He was thinking about the pros. He wanted to play in New York, but the Milwaukee Bucks had won the right to draft him.

They were glad to have me in Milwaukee, but I wasn't the happiest guy in the world to be there. When I arrived it was still warm from Indian summer, but that didn't last long. By October I felt like someone had slammed the freezer door on me. But more than intolerable weather, Milwaukee just wasn't a real city to me. I had lived in only two places, New York and Los Angeles, and this midwestern town had none of the excitement that I had assumed was always in the air like oxygen. For instance, I expected my friends to be the guys in the slick suits and shades because those were the people I was used to seeing in Harlem and Westwood. In my new home I was dealing with, at best, very square business suits; other than that it was the polyester set, which I just could not relate to, or farmers. Farmers!

My being a Muslim didn't help, either. I hadn't made a public pronouncement, everybody still knew me as Lew Alcindor, so I was leading a secret life on top of being from an alien urban culture. People thought I was nuts when I'd ask them to take off their shoes before they entered my apartment. (They knew about Wisconsin winters and minus-twenty-degree nights, and I didn't.)

But they liked me. When I walked on the court the first day I arrived for rookie training camp, I got a three-minute standing ovation. The Bucks were only a year old and had lost more than two thirds of their games in their first season, but all of Wisconsin and upper Michigan and even parts of Minnesota rooted for them as if they were a local high school. The fans came from all over—Delano, Madison, Eau Claire—to see the team play. New York and Los Angeles had the good ethnic diversity; in Milwaukee there were mostly Germans and Polish people, a lot of farmers. I found it difficult, outside of the locker room, working up a good conversation. And, being a Muslim and trying to live by the letter of Muslim law, I found little benefit in extending myself to these people. They were all "disbelievers," and therefore not to be trusted.

The difference between college and the pros came to me fairly quickly. In college, playing two games a week before an audience with whom you have some personal connection, you can prepare and get up for the games emotionally. There always seemed some traditional pride on the line, like some maiden's honor, although maybe you're not the only one who's had her. In the pros you may play as often as four times a week, and the preparation is less emotional than intellectual and physical. The best way to describe it is, overwhelming; you have to devote all your energy and time to your work. If you don't, you lose. It is your work; you are being paid to do this well. With more exertion and less emotion involved, you don't get the exhilaration that you can in college. The pros become a grind, a well-paying grind—you are being paid thousands of dollars a game— but a grind nevertheless. Winning is acceptable. Losing is costing somebody money. In the pros, I found, the game is very rarely fun.

* * *

That autumn, 1971, I changed my name legally from Lew Alcindor to Kareem Abdul-Jabbar. I had lived two lives too long. I knew I was going to take some heat for it, but Muhammad Ali had established a precedent and borne some of the brunt of the attack. There would be the jokes, the unfamiliar Arabic being too difficult or threatening for some people to accept without a fight. There would also be the confusion between my religion and his. This was very important because Ali's religion was a sham to me, and I took mine very seriously. The Muslims and the so-called Black Muslims have very little in common. Rather than go out of my way explaining, however, I chose to make brief, concise statements and insist upon the attention I thought I deserved. I didn't want to be some clown engaging in religious debates with ignoramuses; you didn't hear sportswriters discussing Protestantism with Jerry West. I simply wanted to be called by my legal name and be given the same respect anyone else got. I knew, however, that I would be taunted from a distance. As far as I was concerned, the more distance the better.

* * *

My contract with Milwaukee ended after the next season [1975–76], but I had had enough. Although they offered to buy me a townhouse in New York City and even suggested that I could commute to the games if I would re-sign with the Bucks, it was time to think of a change of venue. I asked to be traded and the Bucks obliged.

It was strange, though. By the time I was about to leave Milwaukee I had finally developed an appreciation of its people. The team owners treated me with respect and paid me well, and the fans turned out to be great. They are the salt of the earth; they show up when you're winning, they show up when you're losing. They come early, stay late, and let you know what's happening while they're there. When I first arrived the fans weren't very knowledgeable about basketball itself, but as the Bucks played it for them they developed rapidly, and by the time I left they were on top of the game. They were a different kind of people than any I'd met before, but I came to know them as generous and good. In New York the fans boo anybody on the opposing team; in Milwaukee they cheer anyone they appreciate. I ended up, much to my surprise, liking Milwaukee. It's too cold for me, but it's too cold for the people who live there too.

I would have played in New York with great pleasure. In fact, I tried to be traded to the Knickerbockers. My friends, my roots, even my family (though I wasn't having much to do with them at the time) were all in the city. Walt Frazier, Earl Monroe, and Bill Bradley were still playing for the Knicks, and it would have been a perfect situation for me.

Unfortunately, the Knicks screwed things up. Rather than trade for me, in which case they would have had to compensate the Bucks with a number of quality players or draft choices, the Knicks chose to try and finesse George McGinnis. George was a high-quality ballplayer working in the ABA who was for the first time becoming available to the NBA. The Knicks did not own the rights to sign him, but they signed him anyway. It was a blatant and obvious power play on the part of the Knicks' management, and the rest of the league squashed them flat, invalidating the deal and penalizing them a first-round draft choice. Meanwhile, they were diverted from signing me. I was very disappointed, but I had to look elsewhere. I could have gone to the Washington Bullets, but I decided against that. Jack Kent Cooke, the owner of the Los Angeles Lakers, had the money for me and the players to exchange with the Bucks, and when that deal was presented I accepted.

Summer in Southern California was a

dream compared to the sub-zero Milwaukee winters. I still had ties in Los Angeles, though it had been six years since I had graduated from UCLA. The big shock when I arrived was to see what it was like living there as an adult rather than as a boy in the closed-in world of the university. It's a town built on celebrity, and I had to learn how that worked.

I took a lot of heat in the papers, supposed to score, rebound, and bring a championship to LA all by myself. I did try. I felt, returning to the city and, it seemed, the public eye, that I had something to prove. I led the league in rebounds and blocked shots and was second in scoring, but the team was the NBA's second to worst in defense, and we finished fourth in our division. I won the MVP for the fourth time, but it was not enough. I've said often that an individual's play cannot carry one team or consistently beat another, and the 1975–76 campaign bears me out; I had the best statistical season of my career, and we missed the playoffs by two games.

* * *

It is the nature of the position of center in the game of basketball as it has developed that one has to almost literally fight for space under the boards or on the court. You know you're going to run into somebody's elbow, trip over an opponent and fall hard on your hip bone, jump in the air and land on somebody's shoulder with your kidney. You can deal with that; it's part of the game. What I've had to contend with for as long as I've played the sport is my opponents' constant attempt to physically punish me and the referees' equally consistent refusal to permit the rules to protect me. Players either want to prevent me from playing successfully or prove themselves against me. Most can't do it within the rules. I take more abuse than anyone in the NBA. After a while I started to dish it back.

Professional basketball is essentially a black sport being run as a white business. All the team owners are white, as are most of the general managers and coaches. (To the NBA's credit, however, it has accepted more blacks in significant management positions than any other major sport.) A great majority of the players are black, which more than anything else creates a marketing problem; the disposable income that pro sports needs in order to thrive is largely in the hands of white people. Blacks play the game in school and in the street, have refined its style and made it a cultural staple, but they haven't got the dollars to fill the arenas or support the television advertisers. Pro basketball is a black game being sold to white people, and the owners, who have serious dollars sunk into the league, are all out to protect their investment.

The other major public relations problem for the NBA is drugs.

Athletes are supposed to be America's heroes. Without ever having volunteered, we are all called upon to personify and uphold the country's honor. Kids look up to us; we are role models for future grandeur. This is nonsense. Athletes should be called upon to be equally as moral as every single individual in society, no more and no less. We are more visible, but not more valuable, than doctors, teachers, cabdrivers and businessmen.

Each man and woman, from the most known to the least, should have the confidence and the strength to create and live by his or her own beliefs and not be led blindly by others who may not be qualified for the job. *Listen* to celebrities; they may be morons.

The uproar over drugs in the NBA is less about morality than it is about commerce. The media makes tremendous money publicizing, analyzing, and criticizing professional sports, and if the product is tarnished, so are the profits. Scandal is good to a degree—it sells newspapers—but there is the constant pressure to maintain the image of cleanliness and not upset the dollar figures. There is also the element of gambling—no doubt about it, millions of dollars are bet annually on pro sports—and an athlete on drugs is more difficult to gauge and make a successful cash determination on than a straight one.

Serious drug use, whether it's pot, cocaine, amphetamines or heroin, will wrestle with your conditioning. Pro basketball demands a physical discipline that is a lot greater than the casual "being in shape." The game itself is grueling, full-tilt exertion for two hours or more, back-and-forth nonstop action. Five minutes up and down the floor at a professional pace is enough to put away most weekend athletes. Then the travel schedule, constant time-zone changes, cramped airplane rides, interrupted sleep, and insistent social temptations all work against your getting any rest. Physical conditioning is an absolute necessity, and if that goes, your game will go with it. Habitual drug users have a hard time in the NBA. Most burn out in a year or two.

* * *

The 1983–84 season had several true and lasting highlights and one serious lowlight. I started the season with a good shot at Wilt Chamberlain's all-time NBA career scoring record and by mid-March it was within reach. I leave the question of whether I'm better than Wilt to the students of the game; that kind of speculation is a fan's birthright. What does it mean? Even now I'm not sure. I still haven't sat back and savored the satisfaction of being the all-time leading scorer. At the time I was keying on the playoffs, which is what playing in the NBA is all about.

There was a lot of pressure, but there was also a lot of warmth. Because of the historical aspect of the record—this thing spanned fifteen years and a lot of people's adolescence and adulthood—all sorts of people wanted to witness and somehow share in the event. With all the media coverage it started to snowball, and when that started happening people who had never paid much attention or shown much respect started to get behind it. "Ah, he's going to do it. What's it about?" I watched at first warily and then with a growing pleasure as basketball fans around the country made me a part of their lives in a way that I really hadn't been before. I truly did feel like I was a part of people's lives. It was a strange and very pleasant experience for me. I'd be driving down the thruway in Los Angeles and some guy in the next lane would recognize me, roll down his window and start weaving down the road yelling, "Pass Wilt, Kareem! Go ahead and do it!" White people, black people, I was finding out who my friends were.

I finally got the record against the Utah Jazz. We were playing in Las Vegas and I had had a hot first half. It was definitely going to be that night. But the Jazz weren't going to roll over; they didn't trick up the whole game to stop me but they weren't going to make it easy, either. They collapsed their defense on me to begin the second half and, just on the brink of the record, I missed several shots in a row. The buckets weren't coming because the Jazz were conscious of it.

Earvin Johnson's whole career has been based around his being a playmaker and helping everyone on his team do their best. He'd said before the game that he wanted the honor of getting the assist on my record-breaking basket, a fine and genuine gesture. But I just kept missing. Finally I set up to the right of the basket and the Jazz started to throw up a double team, almost a triple team. Magic got me the ball and when I saw them coming I stopped. They froze for a split second to see if I was going to pass the ball out for the open jumper, and when they did I went on ahead and put up the hook and— at last—it went in.

The fans went wild, the officials stopped the game and gave me the ball. My mother and father came on the court. It was a wonderful moment.

The next night, at the Forum in Los Angeles, I saw Wilt. The Lakers organized a tribute and during the ceremonies he and I got a chance to speak. Wilt has never gotten the proper respect, people didn't appreciate what Wilt did when he did it; they tossed it off as somebody with superior physical ability doing something that didn't count for much. But I took it seriously, and so did the guys in the NBA, and so does Wilt. Out there on the floor, while other introductions were being made, he leaned over to me privately and said, "I'm glad to see you do it. I'm glad it was you." Wilt would rather his record had stood forever, but he'd been my mentor, had taken an interest in my career before I'd ever had a professional career. It was a very gracious thing to say.

I told the fans in LA that I was happy they could share the moment with me. That was something of a transformation for me, and I think *Giant Steps* had a lot to do with it. While writing and promoting the book, I talked to many more people than I'd ever been comfortable speaking with before. I tried to let people see through my eyes and the results were surprising. Reviewers and readers were startled by my openness and I was pleased by their warm response. They could see that the problems I've dealt with are the same ones they've had to face and that in many ways we are similar, regardless of our physical or cultural differences. I could feel people identifying with me. They approached more easily, and for my part I was more easily approachable. I don't see strangers as attackers any longer, don't feel they're out to tear down what I've accomplished. I can't be everybody's favorite, but at least now people can respect and appreciate what I've done.

ABOUT
KAREEM ABDUL-JABBAR

On April 16, 1947, Ferdinand Lewis Alcindor, Jr., who would become perhaps the greatest basketball player in history, was born in New York City's Harlem.

His mother, Cora, saw schooling as the key to his future. His father, Al, a policeman, wanted him to get good grades—and he did.

In the fourth grade, Lew Alcindor began to play basketball. Although he says he wasn't very good, he did discover his hook shot, which he later perfected as his famous "skyhook." By junior high school, however, he was becoming a good basketball player. During the summer after eighth grade, he began to focus seriously on the game.

In September 1961, Lew entered Power Memorial Academy in New York City. As a 6'10" freshman, he says he had "no strength, zero muscles, and . . . wasn't very aggressive."

Lew's game improved steadily at Power Memorial. He led the team to a 95–6 record and 71 straight victories. They were national champions twice. Lew was an All-City and All-American player for three years in a row.

During these high school years, Lew developed a political consciousness. He saw and felt racial injustice. He studied, learned, and participated in community organizations. He saw for himself the riots in Harlem in the summer of 1964.

That summer, Lew also got to know Wilt Chamberlain, whom he met at a famous Harlem playground tournament, the Rucker Tournament. Also, he became very interested in jazz, and began to spend time in jazz clubs.

In 1965, ready for college, Lew chose the University of California at Los Angeles (UCLA). During the years he played for the UCLA Bruins, they won 88 out of 90 games. They won the national collegiate championship three times. Lew was named the NCAA tournament's most outstanding player all three years.

In the summer of 1967, Lew met Bruce Lee, with whom he studied martial arts until Lee's death five years later. These studies taught Kareem the power of concentration that was an important part of his success.

During his freshman year, Lew read *The Autobiography of Malcolm X*, a book that made him examine his thinking about being black. Back in New York City in the summer of 1968, he began to study Islam and converted to that religion. Also that year, he boycotted the Olympics to protest discrimination against blacks.

After graduating from UCLA in the summer of 1969, Lew signed a basketball contract with the Milwaukee Bucks. In his first professional season, he was named Rookie of the Year.

In 1971, Lewis Alcindor changed his name to Kareem Abdul-Jabbar, which means "generous and powerful servant of Allah." In the same year, he married his first wife, Habiba. In 1972, his first daughter, also named Habiba, was born.

Kareem was chosen the NBA's Most

Valuable Player in 1971 and 1972, an honor that was to be his again in 1974, 1976, 1977, and 1980.

In 1975, Kareem signed with the Los Angeles Lakers, and remained with that team until his retirement in 1989.

In 1976, his first son, Kareem, was born. A few years later, he had a second daughter, Sultana. But his marriage to Habiba ended. He and his second wife, Cheryl, had a son, Amir, in 1980.

Because Kareem is a person who has strong opinions and acts on them, he has sometimes been accused of being cold and difficult. In a 1989 newspaper article, he said: "I was never what you'd call a popular person because of the fact I became a Muslim and I believed in black pride, and people seemed to think I had a chip on my shoulder. I didn't, but . . . I guess it soured my relationship with the press."

In the spring of 1989, at age 42, Kareem Abdul-Jabbar retired from professional basketball. His NBA records (regular season and playoffs) include:

Points scored: 44,149
Field goals made: 18,193
Field goals attempted: 32,729
Games played: 1,797
Seasons played: 20

Kareem has played with many greats of the game. In a *Los Angeles Times* interview, he said: "I was able to play with three of the top five playmakers in NBA history: Oscar [Robertson], Guy Rodgers and Magic [Johnson]. I try to think of a good analogy for that—like if you had a talent for electronics and got a chance to work with Thomas Edison. That's the way I feel."

Kareem was famous for his "skyhook," a graceful, arching, overhand shot that basketball great Bill Russell has called "the most beautiful thing in sports." Sportswriters have called Kareem's moves on the court "artistic." His game was marked by great grace, agility, speed, and elegance.

In the past, Kareem has made movies and commercials. Of the future, Kareem says he will be involved in public relations work with an athletic equipment company and do some acting and movie producing. He also plans to promote literacy among youth and spend more time with his own children.

In recent years, Kareem has let down his guard and become more relaxed and easygoing with the public and the press. In his final games, he was moved by the tributes he received from his fans and his fellow ballplayers.

Retirement Gifts

In the spring of 1989, the NBA organized a farewell tour for Kareem Abdul-Jabbar. Teams he played for and against held ceremonies of tribute, and presented him with gifts, including the following:

Los Angeles Lakers: A 1989 Rolls Royce "Silver Spirit" and a lighted tennis court for his home.

Milwaukee Bucks: A cream and gold Harley-Davidson Electraglide Classic motorcycle, and they retired his No. 33 jersey.

Golden State Warriors: A 24-foot sailboat named "Cap's Sky Hook."

Los Angeles Clippers: A custom-made wet suit and a custom-made surfboard.

New York Knicks: A sterling silver apple.

Boston Celtics: A piece of the Boston Garden floor as a plaque and a $10,000 donation to charity in his name.

Utah Jazz: An 1886 Winchester rifle and custom-made cowboy boots, leather jacket, rattlesnake belt, and hat.

QUESTIONS FOR THE READER

Thinking about the Story

1. What did you think of the selections from *Giant Steps*? What did you like or not like?

2. Are there ways that the events or people in the selections became important or special to you? Write about or discuss them.

3. What do you think were the most important things Kareem Abdul-Jabbar wanted to say?

4. In what ways did the selections answer the questions you had before reading or listening?

5. Were any parts of the selections difficult to understand? If so, you may want to read or listen to them again. You might think about why they were difficult.

Activities

1. Were there any words that were difficult for you in the selections from *Giant Steps*? Go back to these words and try to figure out their meanings. Discuss what you think each word means, and why you made that guess. Discuss with your teacher or another student

how you are going to remember each word. Some ways to remember words are to put them on file cards, or write them in your journal, or create a personal dictionary. Be sure to use the words in your writing in a way that will help you to remember the meaning.

2. How did you help yourself understand the selections? Did you ask yourself questions? What were they? Discuss these questions with other people who have read the same selections, or write about them in your journal.

3. Talking with other people about what you have read can increase your understanding of it. Discussion can help you organize your thoughts, get new ideas, and rethink your original ideas. Discuss your thoughts about the selections with someone else who has read them. Find out if your opinions are the same or different. See if your thoughts change as a result of this discussion.

4. After you finish reading or listening, you might want to write down your thoughts about *Giant Steps*. You could write a book review, or a letter to a friend you think might be interested in Kareem Abdul-Jabbar. You could write your reflections on the book in

your journal, or you could write about topics the book has brought up that you want to explore further.

5. Did reading the selections give you any ideas for your own writing? You might want to write about:

• how you improved a skill or talent you have.

• how your religion has or has not influenced your life.

• your thoughts about drug use in America today.

6. Sometimes organizing information in a visual way can help you better understand or remember it. Look at the timeline of Kareem Abdul-Jabbar's life. You might want to make a timeline of your own.

7. Kareem Abdul-Jabbar has strong opinions about amateur and professional athletics. You might organize a group to discuss the issues surrounding the recruitment, education, and payment of college athletes.

8. If you could talk to Kareem Abdul-Jabbar, what questions would you ask him? You might want to write the questions in your journal.

Kareem Abdul-Jabbar and Peter Knobler, *Selected from GIANT STEPS*, $3.50

Rudolfo A. Anaya, *Selected from BLESS ME, ULTIMA*, $3.50

Maya Angelou, *Selected from I KNOW WHY THE CAGED BIRD SINGS and THE HEART OF A WOMAN*, $3.50

Peter Benchley, *Selected from JAWS*, $3.50

Carol Burnett, *Selected from ONE MORE TIME*, $3.50

Mary Higgins Clark, *Selected from THE LOST ANGEL*, $3.50

Avery Corman, *Selected from KRAMER VS. KRAMER*, $3.50

Bill Cosby, *Selected from FATHERHOOD and TIME FLIES*, $3.50

Louise Erdrich, *Selected from LOVE MEDICINE*, $3.50

Maxine Hong Kingston, *Selected from CHINA MEN and THE WOMAN WARRIOR*, $3.50

Loretta Lynn with George Vecsey, *Selected from COAL MINER'S DAUGHTER*, $3.50

Selected from CONTEMPORARY AMERICAN PLAYS, $3.50

To order, please send your check to Publishing Program, Literacy Volunteers of New York City, 121 Avenue of the Americas, New York, NY 10013. Please add $1.50 per order and .50 per book to cover postage and handling. NY and NJ residents, add appropriate sales tax. Prices subject to change without notice.